THE VIETNAM WAR

PAUL DOWSWELL

WORLD ALMANAC® LIBRARY

Please visit our web site at: www.worldalmanaclibrary.com
For a free color catalog describing World Almanac® Library's
list of high-quality books and multimedia programs,
call 1-800-848-2928 or fax your request to (414) 332-3567.

Library of Congress Cataloging-in-Publication Data

Dowswell, Paul.
    The Vietnam War / by Paul Dowswell.
       p. cm. — (The Cold War)
    Includes bibliographical references and index.
    Summary: Examines the history of conflict in Vietnam, traces the United States involvement from the early 1960s
through 1975, and discusses the consequences of the war on both the United States and Vietnam.
    ISBN 0-8368-5274-5 (lib. bdg.)
    ISBN 0-8368-5279-6 (softcover)
    1. Vietnamese Conflict, 1961-1975—Juvenile literature.   [1. Vietnamese Conflict, 1961-1975.]   I. Title.
II. Series.
DS557.7.D75   2002
959.7—dc21   2001046606

This North American edition first published in 2002 by
World Almanac® Library
330 West Olive Street, Suite 100
Milwaukee, WI 53212 USA

This U.S. edition © 2002 by World Almanac® Library. Original edition published in Great Britain
in 2002 by Hodder Wayland, a division of Hodder Children's Books. Additional end matter
© 2002 by World Almanac® Library.

Series concept: Alex Woolf
Editor: Nicola Edwards
Designer: Derek Lee
Consultant: Dr. J. M. Bourne, Senior Lecturer in Modern History, University of Birmingham
Proofreader and Indexer: Sue Lightfoot
Map illustrator: Nick Hawken
Thanks to Hugh Nolan
World Almanac® Library designer: Scott M. Krall
World Almanac® Library editor: Jim Mezzanotte
World Almanac® Library production: Susan Ashley and Jessica L. Yanke

Picture credits: Associated Press: 47; Camera Press: 16; Corbis: cover, 20; Eye Ubiquitous: cover, title page,
21, 26, 28, 36, 37, 41, 55, 58; Hulton Archive: 39, 48; Pictorial Press Ltd: 4; HWPL: 17 (Andre Malvaux);
Popperfoto: cover, 7, 8, 12, 14, 15, 19, 29, 33, 43, 46, 52, 53, 54; Topham Picturepoint: 5, 10, 22, 25, 27,
30, 34, 40, 44, 51, 56, 57.

Printed in the United States of America

1 2 3 4 5 6 7 8 9 06 05 04 03 02

Contents

CHAPTER ONE

Balcony on the Pacific: Vietnam to 1946

WOUNDS OF WAR

The Vietnam War is fading into history. For many young people, the long and bloody struggle between U.S.-backed South Vietnam and communist North Vietnam is best known through Hollywood movies, such as *Platoon*, *Apocalypse Now*, and *Rambo*. Yet the Vietnam conflict was an American tragedy, and it still casts a long shadow on this country's culture and politics. Over 58,000 U.S. soldiers were killed and more than 304,000 were wounded in Vietnam. For those drafted into the war, Vietnam was often a nightmare that ended adolescence. The dense, tangled landscapes of Southeast Asia, with their strange place names — Da Nang, Khe Sanh, Plain of Jars — and people with radically different language, customs, and dress, must have seemed totally alien to a nineteen-year-old who had just arrived from Ohio or Kansas. These young soldiers often had to contend with the prospect of imminent death from an enemy they rarely, if ever, glimpsed.

Along with personal tragedy, the war also brought national humiliation. While the United States was proving it was the world's most technologically advanced nation by putting men on the Moon, it was also losing a war against a primitive, Third World country whose citizens lived lives that were medieval in their simplicity. When the war ended with

In the movie *Platoon*, Marine sergeant Elias (played by Willem Dafoe) is hunted down by North Vietnamese soldiers. The Hollywood depiction of Vietnam, while compelling, is often not an accurate one.

victory for North Vietnam, the American people had to confront the fact that thousands of lives and billions of dollars had been wasted.

Yet if the United States came away scarred from the war, the cost to Vietnam was far greater. Over three million Vietnamese people lost their lives in the conflict. The U.S. Air Force dropped more bombs on North Vietnam than it did on Japan during World War II. In South Vietnam, U.S. warplanes, intending to deprive North Vietnamese guerilla forces of cover, devastated the environment by spraying chemical defoliants over vast tracts of jungle. In day-to-day fighting, many villages and cities were razed.

THE TV WAR

Journalists covering the Vietnam War had unprecedented access to troops and actual combat, and the brutal reality of the conflict was delivered to the American public on nightly television news bulletins. As the American people witnessed villages burned to the ground and Vietnamese civilians massacred, antiwar protests and civil unrest in the United States escalated.

▼ Vietnamese children, their flesh burning with napalm dropped by U.S. planes, run screaming. This famous photograph came to symbolize the awful effect of the war on Vietnam's civilian population.

"BALCONY ON THE PACIFIC"

Vietnam, which the French called their "balcony on the Pacific," lies on the edge of Southeast Asia. It is bordered by China to the north, Laos and Cambodia to the west, and the South China Sea to the east. A long, narrow country, Vietnam is 1,025 miles (1,650 kilometers) from top to bottom. It has four distinct areas.

The densely populated Red River Delta, where the capital city of Hanoi is located, lies to the north. The large and fertile Mekong Delta, which is home to Ho Chi Minh City (formerly Saigon), lies to the south. In between lies a coastal plain that is heavily populated. The Annamese Cordillera mountain chain takes up two-thirds of the country. Vietnam's climate is generally hot and humid, with monsoon rains and frequent typhoons.

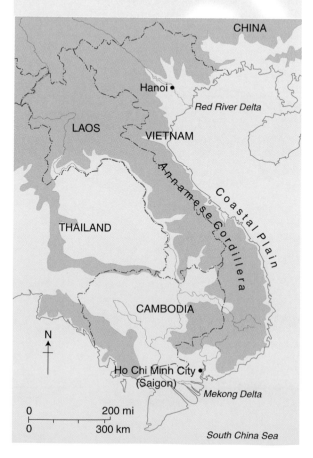

VIETNAM'S PAST

Before U.S. involvement in Vietnam, few Americans could have located Vietnam on a map. Yet this small, mountainous country has a history that began over three thousand years ago, with the emergence of a Vietnamese people in what is now North Vietnam. Chinese warriors invaded this area and ruled it for a thousand years, between 100 B.C. and 900 A.D. Although the Vietnamese repeatedly rebelled against the Chinese occupation, their own culture became inextricably linked with that of China. The Vietnamese, for example, adopted China's Confucian philosophy, with its respect for the past, as well as China's Buddhist religion.

The Chinese occupation also left the Vietnamese people with a deep antagonism towards foreign domination. Unfortunately, the arrival of Europeans in the sixteenth century led to more foreign interference, first by the Portuguese and then later by the French.

FRENCH OCCUPATION

After a long struggle, French troops finally conquered Vietnam in 1883. That same year, the French lumped together Vietnam, Cambodia, and Laos to create the colonial territory of French Indochina. The Vietnamese never stopped rebelling against this foreign occupation, and in the 1930s there were Vietnamese strikes against the French and also executions of rebels by the colonial authorities.

During World War II (1939–1945), France was conquered by Germany and ruled by a Nazi-approved fascist regime. Germany ceded French Indochina to its Axis partner Japan, but administration of the territory continued under the French.

The future leader of North Vietnam, Ho Chi Minh, first came to prominence during the war. Ho had been away from his native Vietnam for thirty years. He had lived in Paris, where he embraced left-wing politics, and he had traveled to such places as the Soviet Union and China. After ending up in Bangkok, Thailand, he made contact with several rebel Vietnamese factions, which he united under his leadership as the "Vietminh." During the war he led the resistance against the French and Japanese, receiving arms and supplies from both China and the United States.

When the war ended, Ho, like many Vietnamese, expected that the French would leave Vietnam along with the defeated Japanese. In a 1945 speech before 100,000 people in the Vietnamese city of Hanoi, Ho declared Vietnam to be an independent country. "The oppressed the world over are wrestling back their independence," he said. "We should not lag behind. Under the Vietminh banner, let us valiantly march forward." France, however, wanted to keep its Far Eastern empire, and it would struggle against Ho and the Vietminh for the next nine years.

When the French finally left Vietnam in 1954, the country was divided into communist North Vietnam and non-communist South Vietnam. Ho became leader of North Vietnam, but until his death in 1969, he would seek to unite the entire country into one communist nation.

HO CHI MINH (1890–1969)

Ho Chi Minh — his name translates to "he who enlightens" in Vietnamese — led the Vietnamese communists from 1945 until his death in 1969. A slight figure, Ho suffered from tuberculosis, malaria, and dysentery, but he was an incredibly resilient and charismatic man. Originally named Nguyen Tat Thanh, Ho was the son of a teacher. As a young man, he taught briefly, then became a sailor and traveled the world. After World War I, he settled in Paris, where he came into contact with leftist political groups. Ho was greatly inspired by the communist revolution in Russia and became a founding member of the French Communist Party.

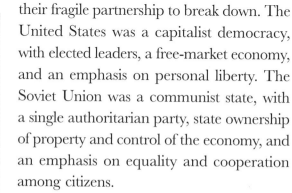

CHAPTER TWO

First Indochina War, 1946–1954

COLONIAL EXPLOITATION

The Vietnamese suffered under French colonial rule. When the French arrived in the 1840s, the literacy rate in Vietnam was eighty percent — a figure that would have put many European nations to shame. By the time the French left, however, only twenty percent of Vietnam was literate. The fact that powerful Saigon gangsters supported the French regime says much about its corruption and exploitation of the Vietnamese people.

WRONG PLACE, WRONG TIME

After World War II, France's efforts to gain back control of Vietnam had little support in the United States. Vietnam, however, was unfortunately in the wrong place at the wrong time. Events unfolding in other parts of the world would have tragic consequences for the tiny country.

The United States and the Soviet Union fought together against the Nazis, but once the war ended, in 1945, the contrasting ideologies of these two new "superpowers" caused their fragile partnership to break down. The United States was a capitalist democracy, with elected leaders, a free-market economy, and an emphasis on personal liberty. The Soviet Union was a communist state, with a single authoritarian party, state ownership of property and control of the economy, and an emphasis on equality and cooperation among citizens.

Mutual distrust between the two nations quickly escalated into the Cold War, a rivalry that involved threats and stalemates

Eve of the Cold War. British prime minister Churchill, U.S. president Truman, and Soviet premier Stalin meet at the end of World War II. Allied with the United States and Britain during the war, the Soviet Union then became an adversary.

but never reached actual armed conflict. On one side stood the United States and other Western democracies, such as Britain and France; on the other side stood the Soviet Union and a growing number of Soviet-backed communist countries in Eastern Europe. The United States sought to stop the spread of communism, while the Soviet Union, which lost more than 20 million people fighting the Nazis, sought to protect and increase its power in the world.

If Ho Chi Minh had simply been a nationalist who wanted independence for his country, thirty years of bloody conflict might never have occurred. Ho and his followers, however, were communists. They found support from the Soviet Union and, as the 1940s drew to a close, another important communist regime.

COMMUNIST CONSPIRACY VS. "BATTERED KITE"

From the start, the United States was suspicious of Ho Chi Minh and the Vietminh and automatically assumed that Ho's objectives in Vietnam were part of a wider communist conspiracy to take over the whole of Asia. In 1950, a National Security Council report stated:

"The threat of communist aggression against Indochina is only one phase of anticipated communist plans to seize all of Southeast Asia."

Other U.S. policy makers, however, were more ambivalent about the situation in Vietnam. That same year, another State Department official who was concerned with increasing U.S. interest in Vietnam remarked:

"Whether the French like it or not, independence is coming to Indochina. Why, therefore, do we tie ourselves to the tail of their battered kite?"

DOMINO THEORY

In 1949, Chinese communist forces, led by Mao Tse-tung, defeated the nationalist government and took control of China. Ho and the Vietminh now had a powerful communist neighbor who was sympathetic to their objectives and politics.

This scenario alarmed the United States. During the Cold War, which lasted until the collapse of the Soviet Union in 1991, it considered communism to be a virus that could spread from one nation to another. This view was expressed as the domino theory. The theory held that if one country fell to communists, then other countries in that region would each fall in turn, like a row of dominoes.

To stop communism, the United States followed a broad policy of containment. With this policy, the United States sought to prevent — by military force, if necessary — the spread of communism to non-communist countries.

▲ In what appears to be a staged photograph taken for communist propaganda purposes, U.S. soldiers surrender to North Korean soldiers during the Korean War.

WAR IN KOREA

No sooner had the communists seized power in China than an international conflict broke out on their doorstep. The Korean peninsula, which runs parallel with Japan and also borders China, had been divided after World War II, in much the same way as would soon happen in Vietnam. The northern half of the peninsula became communist North Korea, while the southern half became non-communist South Korea.

In 1950 North Korea, backed with Soviet arms, attacked South Korea. A combination of U.S. and United Nations coalition troops then came to South Korea's aid. The U.S.-UN forces drove back the North Koreans and swept north all the way to the Chinese border, at which point Chinese troops joined the war on the North's side. After much fighting, the two sides settled into a stalemate near the original division of the peninsula. An armistice was signed in 1953, and an uneasy truce settled on North and South Korea.

COLD WAR ATTITUDES

The United States feared a similar situation in Vietnam. Although they regarded France's efforts to control the country with distaste, they provided the French with four billion dollars of military aid. This aid had originally been meant to support the French government against a strong communist opposition in France, but once China became communist and the Korean War broke out, Vietnam assumed new importance. Due to the Cold War attitudes shaping U.S. foreign policy, the North Vietnamese struggle against French colonialism was now seen as a communist conspiracy to dominate all of Southeast Asia.

FRANCE TAKES ACTION

France had its own reasons for not wanting to let go of Vietnam. After the national humiliation of its Nazi occupation during World War II, it wanted to regain some of its previous prestige and power. French troops began an active campaign against Ho's Vietminh forces, driving them from Hanoi and other cities, such as the port of Haiphong, where a French navy bombardment killed 6,000 residents.

Ho's military commander, a former Hanoi law student named Vo Nguyen Giap, quickly discovered that when Vietminh forces fought the French in conventional battles they always suffered heavy casualties. Changing tactics, he began a campaign of guerrilla warfare. His troops set ambushes, planted mines, and carried out hit-and-run raids and sniper attacks. They whittled away at the French forces, and in the process broke both the morale of the soldiers and support of the war by the French people. Nonetheless, the conflict between the French and the Vietminh dragged on for years.

French military leaders eventually decided that they had to force the Vietminh forces out into the open. In March 1954, a major armed camp was established in the northwest corner of Vietnam, in a remote valley called Dien Bien Phu. At this camp, 16,500 French soldiers dug themselves in and waited for the Vietminh to attack.

A FRENCH PERSPECTIVE

In 1954, French general Thomas Trapnall reported on the situation in Indochina:

"It is a savage conflict fought in a fantastic country in which the battle may be waged one day in waist-deep muddy rice paddies or later in an impenetrable mountainous jungle. The sun saps the vitality of friend and foe alike ... It is a war with no immediate solution, a politico-military chess game in which the players sit thousands of miles distant — in Paris, Washington, Peking and Moscow ..."

11

FRANCE DEFEATED

The Vietminh did attack, but not in the way the French had expected. Together with thousands of Chinese volunteers, the Vietminh hauled large artillery up to the high hills that surrounded Dien Bien Phu, hiding the artillery in caves to keep it safe from air attack. French pilots were also frustrated by the constant mist that settled on the hills, making any target extremely difficult to see.

▼ French soldiers await another attack by Vietminh troops at Dien Bien Phu. All around them are supplies dropped into the besieged camp by parachute.

In their fortified camp, the French ground troops were pulverized by a constant bombardment of artillery fire. Despite the heavy shelling, the French hung on to Dien Bien Phu, while the Vietminh took heavy losses in frontal assaults. Then the Vietminh began digging tunnels under the perimeter of the camp. During lulls in the shelling, exhausted French troops heard the clattering of shovels as the Vietminh burrowed beneath their feet, occasionally bursting out of the ground in desperate suicide attacks.

After two months, the French surrendered. The battle of Dien Bien Phu had cost them the war, and they gave up their colony. In the Indochina conflict, 75,000 French soldiers died from combat or disease — a much greater number than U.S. losses in the next two decades. Still, Vietnam had suffered a far heavier sacrifice, with 300,000 Vietnamese having died in the struggle for independence. They may have lacked the technology and economic power of the French, but the Vietnamese people had proved they had the drive and determination to defeat forces far stronger than themselves.

THE GENEVA ACCORDS

The Indochina war ended with a conference in Geneva, Switzerland, and a settlement called the Geneva Accords. Vietminh leaders, now calling themselves citizens of the Democratic Republic of Vietnam, as well as representatives of the non-communist Vietnamese, attended the Geneva conference with representatives from France, the United States, the Soviet Union, China, and Britain.

The Vietminh assumed their victory over the French would give them control of the whole country, but they were mistaken. Despite fears by the United States and its allies of a worldwide communist conspiracy, the Soviet and Chinese representatives urged the Vietminh to sign a settlement that would be acceptable to the United States, France, and Britain.

After ten weeks of wrangling, an agreement was reached. France would give up its former colony, and Vietnam would be divided, temporarily, into the communist North and the non-communist South. Elections were supposed to be held within two years to decide who would rule a united Vietnam.

A DIVIDED VIETNAM

Following the Geneva Accords settlement that was reached in 1954, Vietnam was temporarily divided into North Vietnam and South Vietnam, with elections deciding who would rule the entire country to be held within two years. The area marking the division between North and South was called the Demilitarized Zone, or DMZ.

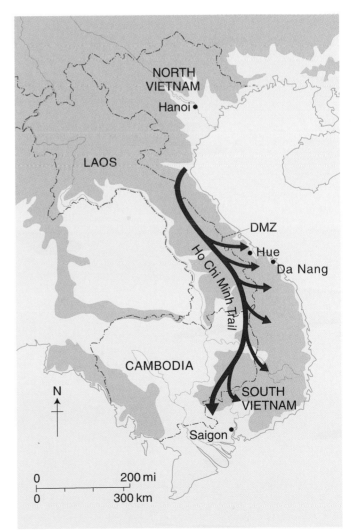

CHAPTER THREE

Second Indochina War, 1954–1963

COLD WAR POLITICS

If the Vietminh were mistaken about their assumption that they would rule all of Vietnam after driving out the French, they were also mistaken in believing that the new division between North and South would soon disappear. Once again, the realities of the Cold War and U.S. foreign policy would have a powerful influence on the fate of Vietnam.

When the last French troops left Vietnam in 1955, the United States rushed to fill their place — at least in South Vietnam. Rather than an occupying colonial power, however, the United States saw itself as a friendly "big brother" who would protect the South from the North's communist intentions. The course Vietnam would take was now irrevocably bound up with the Cold War politics of the 1950s. Without the Cold War, the United States might never have backed the South Vietnamese government so strongly.

THE COMMUNIST THREAT

In the 1950s, American hostility towards communism reached intense heights, especially after the Soviet Union began to build nuclear weapons to rival those of the United States.

Beginning in 1950, U.S. senator Joseph McCarthy whipped up anticommunist hysteria by instigating a series of "witch-hunts" to root out communist sympathizers among government officials. The witch-hunts ended in 1954, but a fear of spreading communism did not. U.S. leaders still pursued a rigid foreign policy that saw the world divided into communist and non-communist nations.

▲ U.S. government official Alger Hiss, who was accused of being a communist. Like many other officials, as well as politicians and media figures, his career was ruined by such accusations.

Within this frigid Cold War atmosphere, North and South Vietnam each settled into a new post-Geneva Accords existence. In the North, Ho Chi Minh was the undisputed leader of a communist regime. In the South, a man named Ngo Dinh Diem was appointed prime minister.

DIEM LEADS SOUTH VIETNAM

Diem, as he was generally known, had taken on an immensely difficult job. He had no effective armed forces, no police force, and no civil service. His country's weak economy had been further undermined by 900,000 refugees fleeing North Vietnam's communist regime. Diem also had many enemies. Ho Chi Minh still enjoyed strong support in the South, especially in the countryside. In addition, two armed religious groups known as the Cao Dai and the Hoa Hao, as well as gangster private armies, also threatened his regime. Lastly, Diem was a Catholic in a predominantly Buddhist society.

South Vietnam needed a capable leader who could deal with the country's many problems and unite its various factions. Diem, however, was not that leader. While he took decisive, if violent, action against both the religious groups and the gangsters, he killed many innocent people in the process, stirring even more opposition to him.

Perhaps Diem's most critical failing, for a leader with such little support, was his refusal to share power with other political groups. Instead, he placed members of his own family in important political positions. His brother Ngo Dinh Nhu, for example, was head of the secret police. Nhu was Diem's confidant and closest adviser. He was also a drug addict.

NGO DINH DIEM (1901–1963)

Diem was a haughty, solemn man. U.S. journalist Stanley Karnow described him as *"a rotund little figure whose feet barely touched the floor when he sat on the elegant chairs … of the palace. He looked as fragile as porcelain, with delicate features and ivory skin, but his eyes projected a fanatical faith in his crusade."*

In 1961, U.S. vice president Lyndon Johnson described Diem as *" … the Churchill of the decade … in the vanguard of those leaders who stand for freedom."* When Stanley Karnow asked Johnson if he had meant what he said, the vice president replied *"****, Diem's the only boy we got out there."*

VIETNAM DIVIDED

U.S. leaders had serious reservations about Diem, but he was staunchly anticommunist and there seemed to be no one suitable to replace him. Diem was encouraged by U.S. advisers to forget about the Geneva Accords elections, which he would almost certainly have lost. Instead, with U.S. assistance, he set about establishing South Vietnam as a separate independent nation.

North Vietnam's Chinese and Soviet allies sought to avoid drawing the United States into a major war in Vietnam, which they knew was likely to happen if the North attacked the South. They convinced Ho Chi Minh not to take action against Diem's clear breach of the Geneva treaty. For the time being, Ho waited to see if the South Vietnamese people would rise up against Diem's regime and topple it themselves.

▲ Guerrilla forces from North Vietnam bring supplies down the Ho Chi Minh Trail. The low-tech approach of North Vietnam was ultimately more effective than the United States' reliance on sophisticated weapons and transportation.

"DENOUNCE A COMMUNIST"

With a characteristic lack of political skill, Diem attempted to strengthen his position by attacking Ho's supporters in the South. When he initiated a "denounce a communist" campaign, pro-communists in South Vietnam organized into fighting groups to defend themselves. These groups became known as the "Vietcong" — a term that would be used to describe South Vietnamese communist rebels throughout the war.

By 1957, fighting between these rebels and South Vietnam's Army of the Republic of Vietnam, or "ARVN," troops had resulted in over 2,000 deaths and the arrest of over 65,000 South Vietnamese that the government suspected of being communists. The rebels retaliated against Diem's regime by assassinating local government officials and carrying out guerrilla skirmishes against the ARVN.

As fighting continued, Ho Chi Minh's regime began to actively supply the communist rebels in South Vietnam with both armed support and equipment. North Vietnam established a ramshackle but effective supply route, dubbed the "Ho Chi Minh Trail" (see page 23), to assist the rebels. In addition to passing from North Vietnam deep into South Vietnam, the supply route also intruded into neighboring Laos and Cambodia.

By the end of 1957, the conflict in South Vietnam had escalated into civil war. Diem responded by ordering the formation of "agrovilles" — fortified villages, far from communist-controlled areas, to which peasants were forcibly relocated in order to isolate them from communist rebels. This clumsy policy made Diem even more unpopular. By the end of 1960, the communist rebels and other groups opposed to Diem had formed a broad coalition, which they called the National Liberation Front.

JOHN F. KENNEDY (1917–1963)

Following Dwight Eisenhower's staid, conservative presidency, John F. Kennedy and his wife Jackie brought a youthful glamour to the White House. Kennedy was the son of Joseph Kennedy, a millionaire businessman who had been British ambassador during World War II. During the 1960 presidential elections, Kennedy's opponent, Richard Nixon, accused him of being "soft on communism," but Kennedy actually believed that the United States had to stop what he called "the onrushing tide of communism" from engulfing all of Asia.

▼ President Kennedy and his wife Jackie (left and center, respectively) greet guests at a White House social event. Vice President Lyndon Johnson stands behind the First Lady.

A NEW PRESIDENT

In the United States, anxiety over the situation in Vietnam began to grow among government leaders. The newly elected president, John F. Kennedy, took the same view as his predecessor, Dwight Eisenhower. If Diem's regime was toppled, then all of Vietnam would fall under communist control. According to the domino theory, communism would then spread like a plague to neighboring Burma, India, and even Africa. With so much at stake, President Kennedy decided that Diem's regime had to be supported at all costs.

MORE U.S. INVOLVEMENT

The United States now increased its involvement in South Vietnam. U.S. military advisors began training the ARVN, and the Central Intelligence Agency, or CIA, which was responsible for U.S. foreign intelligence, began organizing anticommunist groups within South Vietnam. In addition, 3,700 "strategic hamlets" were established in the countryside. Like Diem's agrovilles, the hamlets were meant to isolate peasants from antigovernment forces, and they were also meant to provide strongholds in the countryside's rebel-controlled territories.

No matter how much assistance the United States provided, it could not buy support for Diem among the people. By 1963 the battle against the communist forces was going so badly that 2,600 strategic hamlets had been destroyed.

In the end, however, South Vietnam's Buddhists, and not its communists, led to Diem's downfall. Diem had a brother, Ngo Dihn Thuc, who was a Roman Catholic archbishop. A powerful and arrogant man, Thuc forbade the display of Buddhist flags during a Buddhist holiday, provoking demonstrations in the mostly Buddhist country. Troops were called out, and they shot and killed several Buddhist monks. Buddhist temples were also raided and martial law was declared.

BLACK-AND-WHITE PERSPECTIVES

On both sides of the Vietnam conflict, a clash of ideologies discouraged any real understanding or compromise.

Ho Chi Minh told his people that victory by the North would bring " ... *an era of right and justice ... in the struggle of civilization against barbarism."*

President Kennedy described the United States' crusade against communism as *"a struggle for supremacy between two conflicting ideologies: freedom under God versus ruthless, godless tyranny."*

BUDDHIST PROTESTS

Some outraged Buddhists then burned themselves to death publicly as a form of protest, and photographs of the acts immediately spread around the world. Diem's sister-in-law, Madame Nhu, dismissed the protests as "Buddhist barbecues," speaking volumes about the moral fiber of Diem's family. "Let them burn," she was quoted as saying, "and we shall clap our hands."

Diem's quarrel with the Buddhists was the last straw. U.S. officials in Vietnam were informed of an army plot to remove Diem, but they did nothing. On November 1, 1963, ARVN troops ousted Diem, and, along with his brother Nhu, he was executed. While the U.S. government expressed shock at the killings, it held out hope for a new, more effective leader.

More shocks were on the horizon. On November 22, 1963, President Kennedy was assassinated. If Kennedy supported U.S. involvement in Vietnam, his successor, Vice President Lyndon Baines Johnson, would escalate it to new heights.

▼ As residents in Saigon look on with almost nonchalant curiosity, another Buddhist monk burns himself to death as a protest against religious discrimination. Diem's feud with Buddhists in South Vietnam led directly to his overthrow and execution.

CHAPTER FOUR

Search and Destroy:
Full U.S. Involvement,
1964–1967

▲ President Johnson's hopes for far-reaching social reforms were dashed by the Vietnam conflict, which cost money and lives and became hugely unpopular.

JOHNSON'S DILEMMA

President Johnson may best be remembered as the man who plunged the United States into a much deeper involvement in Vietnam. When Johnson first came to power, however, he was mostly concerned with bettering the lives of the American people, not entangling the country in a foreign war.

With his "Great Society" domestic program, Johnson sought to fight poverty and improve opportunities for housing, health care, and education, but he still had to deal with Cold War politics. South Vietnam was on the verge of communist domination, and according to U.S. foreign policy, communism could not be allowed to spread in Southeast Asia. Johnson first tried to support South Vietnam in a way that would minimize public opposition and allow him to push through his Great Society legislation. In the end, his strategy failed.

When Johnson was sworn in as president in November 1963, the situation in South Vietnam could not have been worse. Although the government forces had more troops and better supplies, the communist rebels controlled over a third of the country and had gone beyond guerrilla warfare to direct attacks on ARVN troops. Johnson's military advisers predicted an imminent collapse of the anticommunist regime in South Vietnam, and the president believed he had no option but to prop up the country with more U.S. support.

THE GULF OF TONKIN RESOLUTION

Johnson needed to convince the American people that he had a good reason for expanding U.S. involvement in South

Vietnam. He found his justification in August 1964, when North Vietnamese patrol boats fired on U.S. Navy ships stationed off the coast of North Vietnam in the Gulf of Tonkin. Since the ships were providing cover for commando raids by South Vietnamese forces, the North Vietnamese believed they had a legitimate reason for firing. Johnson, however, convinced Congress that the attack was proof of North Vietnam's intention to wage war against the United States. The U.S. Constitution states that only Congress can declare war. To support Johnson, however, Congress passed the Gulf of Tonkin resolution, which essentially gave the president the power to authorize military action without a congressional declaration of war.

Johnson understood that greater U.S. involvement would most likely mean greater U.S. casualties, which would not be popular with the American people. To minimize casualties, Johnson decided to rely upon the U.S. Air Force, which was arguably the most powerful and sophisticated fighting machine on the planet. Johnson hoped that U.S. bombers could quickly destroy North Vietnam's ability to wage war, with minimal loss of American lives. To achieve this goal, "Operation Rolling Thunder" began in March 1965.

THE "GREAT SOCIETY"

President Johnson's vision of a "Great Society," which involved discouraging racial prejudice, reducing poverty, and improving health care and education for all citizens, was undermined by the conflict in Vietnam.

"In your time we have the opportunity to move not only toward the rich society and the powerful society, but upward to the Great Society."

PRESIDENT LYNDON JOHNSON, IN A SPEECH TO UNIVERSITY OF MICHIGAN STUDENTS, 1964

"The Great Society has been shot down on the battlefield of Vietnam."

CIVIL RIGHTS LEADER MARTIN LUTHER KING, 1967

▼ U.S. Navy personnel prepare for the launch of an F-4 Phantom bomber from the deck of the USS *Midway*, stationed near the mainland of North Vietnam. U.S. airpower was effective, but it was never a deciding factor in the outcome of the war.

ROLLING THUNDER

At the time, "Operation Rolling Thunder" was the most massive bombing campaign in history. U.S. planes unloaded thousands of tons of bombs on North Vietnam, destroying factories, roads, bridges, and supplies. The campaign inflicted approximately $340 million worth of damage and killed thousands of Vietnamese. Summing up the official U.S. attitude towards the campaign, U.S. Air Force general Curtis E. LeMay said, "They've got to draw in their horns and stop their aggression, or we're going to bomb them back into the Stone Age."

General LeMay, however, did not understand that North Vietnam was already one of the most low-tech nations on Earth. Essentially an agricultural society, North Vietnam had the most rudimentary industry and transportation systems. (Today the main railway line between North and South Vietnam is still a single track.) "Operation Rolling Thunder" might have devastated an industrialized nation, but the North Vietnamese quickly bounced back from the bombardment. They rebuilt roads, railways, and factories and received aid from China and the Soviet Union to make up for the losses of arms and other supplies.

▼ The first U.S. combat troops spill out of landing craft on the beaches of Da Nang in March 1965. Within four years, over a half million U.S. troops would be stationed in Vietnam.

THE HO CHI MINH TRAIL

The Ho Chi Minh Trail perfectly illustrated the North Vietnamese attributes of low-tech resourcefulness and steely determination. Stretching from North Vietnam deep into South Vietnam, this makeshift route supplied arms, provisions, and North Vietnamese soldiers to the communist rebels in South Vietnam throughout the war. Traveling the length of the trail took between two to six months. Trucks sometimes transported troops and equipment, but most Vietnamese using the trail walked or pushed supplies on bicycles. Up to one in five who set out for South Vietnam died along the trail, either from exhaustion, illness, or frequent air attacks.

During the course of the conflict, North Vietnamese air defenses improved, and their fighter planes, missiles, and anti-aircraft guns brought down over 700 U.S. planes. (The greatest number of U.S. prisoners of war during the conflict would be aircrew.)

"The Americans thought the more bombs they dropped, the quicker we would fall to our knees and surrender. But the bombs heightened rather than dampened our spirit."

NORTH VIETNAMESE DOCTOR, TON THAT TUNG

U.S. COMBAT TROOPS

During the 1964 presidential election, Johnson had made a promise to the American people. "We are not about to send American boys nine or ten thousand miles away from home," he said, "to do what Asian boys ought to be doing for themselves." In 1965, however, the new U.S. involvement in Vietnam resulted in Johnson's promise being broken.

In order to accommodate all the U.S. planes now flying missions, new U.S. bases had to be built in South Vietnam. General William Westmoreland, commander of U.S. forces in Vietnam, believed that ARVN troops would not be able to defend these bases, and he requested that U.S. soldiers handle the job. U.S. combat troops first landed in Vietnam in March 1965. Soldiers from U.S. allies also arrived, including 8,000 Australian and 60,000 South Korean troops.

U.S. INVOLVEMENT DEEPENS

Believing that the South Vietnamese army could not win the war against the communist rebels, U.S. military officials wanted to send in more U.S. troops. As General Earle Wheeler, Chairman of the Joint Chiefs of Staff, commented, "You must carry the fight to the enemy. No one ever won a battle sitting on his ass." At the end of 1964, there were 23,000 U.S. soldiers in Vietnam. By 1967, the number had risen to 535,000.

Unfortunately, the increase in U.S. troops created a vicious circle. The ARVN forces had always been reluctant to fight, and as U.S. involvement increased, many soldiers in the South Vietnamese army believed that U.S. soldiers would do their fighting for them. Every year, one third of the ARVN deserted.

"SEARCH AND DESTROY"

To locate and eradicate rebel groups in South Vietnam, General Westmoreland pursued a strategy called "search and destroy" that used all the sophisticated weaponry at the United States' disposal. Helicopters ferried troops to remote landing zones in the country where enemy forces were reportedly operating. The troops dropped there kept in constant radio contact with headquarters. An officer in the field could order an air strike from an offshore carrier with ground support aircraft, and have the strike delivered within minutes.

THE FIVE O'CLOCK NEWS

After seeing the Vietnam conflict on television back home, many new soldiers found combat there to be terrifying yet oddly familiar.

"I heard some Skyhawks [U.S. jet planes] coming in dropping bombs ... It was just like the five o'clock news back home. There were some gunships and a 34 [U.S. helicopter] comes in and all of a sudden it bursts into flames and drops straight out of the sky ... All of a sudden this guy comes running up ... He says 'Saddle up, we're going to help ...' I thought 'Holy ****! Here I am a spectator, now I'm going to be in the middle of this thing.' I was scared beyond description."

LANCE CORPORAL GARY CONNOR

AGENT ORANGE

These U.S. planes could incinerate enemy troops with napalm — a gasoline-based burning fluid — or strafe them with machine guns that could fire over a hundred rounds a second. Eventually, U.S. planes also sprayed vast tracts of Vietnam (3.6 million acres in all) with herbicides such as Agent Orange, which destroyed the dense rain forest that communist guerrillas used for cover and sustenance.

▲ A once-dense forest has been turned into a dusty wasteland to make a landing zone for U.S. helicopters. These aircraft could transport troops into battle and evacuate wounded men quickly, but they were all too easily shot down by enemy fire.

▲ As their transport helicopter returns to base, soldiers of the U.S. 73rd Airborne Division begin a nerve-wracking patrol in Vietcong territory.

SUCCESSION OF LEADERS: NGUYEN VAN THIEU (1923–)

Diem's assassination in November 1963 by no means brought political stability to South Vietnam. Instead, four different heads of state followed in quick succession until February 1965, when the commander of South Vietnam's air force, Nguyen Cao Ky, became leader. In September 1967, Ky was himself succeeded by Nguyen Van Thieu, who stayed in power until the collapse of South Vietnam in 1975.

A Catholic who had been an officer in the French colonial army, Thieu also received military training in the United States and had close ties to the West. His regime, however, was described by William Bundy, one of President Johnson's closest advisers, as "absolutely the bottom of the barrel." Thieu was thoroughly corrupt and took millions of dollars of gold with him when he fled South Vietnam in 1975.

A HOLLOW VICTORY

At first, Westmoreland's campaign appeared to be succeeding. The United States suffered 13,500 casualties between 1965 and 1967, but enemy casualties during that time numbered nearly 200,000. For U.S. military officials, the United States' reliance on technological superiority was both winning the war and keeping their own casualties low.

In the end, however, Westmoreland's strategy failed to defeat the communist rebels. U.S. soldiers could clear an area of communist forces, but they would always return within a few months.

The communist soldiers who fought in South Vietnam had two great advantages over their enemies. First, most of the time they had the support of the peasants in the areas where they operated, and could melt into anonymity whenever hostile troops approached. Second, they could decide when and where to attack. Throughout the Vietnam conflict, nine out of ten encounters between the communist rebels and the non-communist forces were initiated by the communists. U.S. and South Vietnamese troops searched for the enemy, but more often than not they only found them when they were attacked.

THE DRAFT

A deepening U.S. involvement in Vietnam meant that the size of the armed forces had to be increased. Beginning in 1965, the U.S. government instituted the "draft," which was selective service in the armed forces for male citizens between the ages of eighteen and twenty-five. Since college students were allowed deferments from the draft so they could complete their educations, the draft mostly called upon the country's working class.

▼ As the draft widened its net, it became increasingly unpopular among the country's young people, who often included the burning of their draft cards (below) in demonstrations against the war.

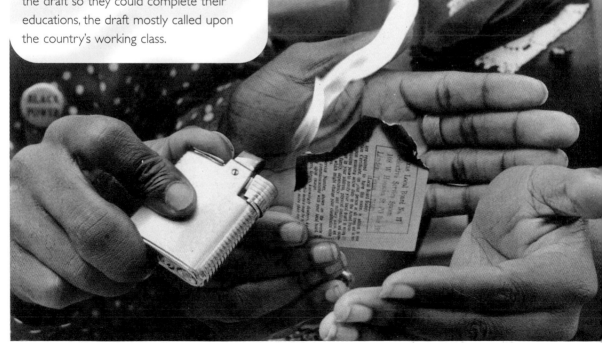

CHAPTER FIVE

The Tet Offensive and Its Aftermath, 1968

KHE SANH

In 1968, the communists laid to waste any U.S. notions of easy victory in Vietnam. The year started with several attacks on isolated U.S. bases. Worst hit was Khe Sanh, a Marine camp near the North Vietnamese border that was besieged for several months. Although Khe Sanh was not all that important for the U.S. campaign, it became a symbol of the United States' refusal to be driven out of Vietnam.

General Westmoreland was determined that the base would not fall. He ordered 6,000 troops airlifted into the base, and he also ordered the most intense aerial bombardment in the history of warfare. In all, B-52 bombers dropped 100,000 tons of bombs on five square miles around the base, in an effort to destroy the invisible enemy in the surrounding jungle.

President Johnson was likewise obsessed with Khe Sanh. In a basement room in the White House, Johnson's staff constructed a model of the base, and at night the president would pace around in his dressing gown as he read the latest battle reports. The communists ultimately gave up on Khe Sanh, and despite all the attention the base had been given, it was then dismantled.

▼ The U.S. stronghold at Khe Sanh in early 1968. Safe inside the perimeter of the base, U.S. soldiers consume their rations amidst the base's debris.

THE TET OFFENSIVE

Unfortunately, there was more to come from the communists. On January 30, 1968, North Vietnam launched a major assault on South Vietnam. Named the Tet offensive for the Vietnamese lunar New Year being celebrated at the time, the assault involved 84,000 troops from both Vietcong forces and the North Vietnamese Army (NVA).

North Vietnam chose the day of its offensive well. Tet celebrations were a national holiday in Vietnam, and the South Vietnamese were caught off guard. During the Tet celebrations it was customary to set off firecrackers and other fireworks. In Saigon, residents later recalled hearing the usual celebratory fireworks after midnight, then realizing that many of the bangs they heard were actually gunshots and exploding mortar shells.

Shifting their focus from South Vietnam's countryside to its urban centers, the communists attacked thirty-six major cities and towns. In Saigon, communist commandos destroyed the radio station and attacked such high-profile targets as the airport, the presidential palace, and the headquarters of the South Vietnamese army. Most alarming of all — at least for the United States — was the fact that they also assaulted the U.S. embassy. A commando unit of nineteen men broke into the embassy grounds and held out for several hours, and one or two even managed to enter the embassy itself before being killed. U.S. ambassador Ellsworth Bunker was asleep in his home nearby, but the night-duty officer felt it necessary to lock himself in the embassy code room to escape the attackers.

▲ High above Vietnam, a U.S. B-52 bomber spews out its explosive cargo. No place on Earth has been more heavily bombed than Vietnam.

VO NGUYEN GIAP (1911-)

The architect of the Tet offensive was Ho Chi Minh's right-hand man, General Vo Nguyen Giap. A tiny, elflike figure, Giap was North Vietnam's vice-premier and minister of defense, and he had transformed the Vietminh guerrillas into a national fighting force capable of defeating both the French and U.S. armies. Giap was blessed with soldiers willing to make great sacrifices for their homeland. Describing his overall strategy, he said, "another twenty years, even a hundred years, as long as it took to win, regardless of cost."

 Among the ruins of their city, citizens of Hue attempt a return to normal life in March 1968. Hue was a main target during the Tet offensive, and fighting in the city created 100,000 refugees.

HUE

Besides the attack on Saigon, the most significant assault of the Tet offensive was the attack on the ancient city of Hue, close to the North Vietnamese border. For three weeks, 7,500 communist troops seized control of parts of Hue. They acted with great brutality, executing up to 5,000 government officials, as well as other citizens who had links with the United States and the South Vietnamese regime. The communists lost control of Hue, but during the fighting the city was destroyed, and 100,000 of its citizens became refugees. The Tet offensive eventually created a million refugees.

In many ways, the Tet offensive was a disaster for the communists. While U.S. and South Vietnamese losses from the offensive totaled 3,400, in contrast over 30,000 North Vietnamese and Vietcong soldiers died, and all of the territory they seized was lost by the summer. The Vietcong forces would never regain their former strength.

The communists had hoped that, given some assistance, the people of South Vietnam would rise up against their government. This rebellion never occurred. Whether through fear, dislike, or indifference, most South Vietnamese civilians neither supported nor joined the communist soldiers that were in their midst.

STALEMATE

The Tet offensive did, however, have a huge impact on U.S. involvement in Vietnam, an impact best illustrated by a remark made by CBS news anchorman Walter Cronkite: "What the hell is going on? I thought we were winning the war!" While Cronkite's comment was not broadcast, the trusted television personality did go on to tell his audience that, in his view, "the bloody experience of Vietnam is to end in stalemate."

General Westmoreland maintained that the Tet offensive had been a defeat for the communists. In reality, however, Tet proved that the United States was not winning its war in Vietnam. Despited its sophisticated technology and large number of troops, the United States could not eradicate the enemy. For many government officials, Tet was the turning point of the war — the moment when they realized the United States could not win in Vietnam. The billions of dollars spent on propping up South Vietnam had still left it weak and open to defeat, and so-called "pacification" programs meant to destroy communist forces had been a failure.

"TOO DUMB TO LIE DOWN"

In his classic account of the Vietnam war, *Dispatches*, journalist Michael Herr describes the impact of the Tet offensive:

"We took a huge collective nervous breakdown ... every American in Vietnam got a taste. Vietnam was a dark room full of heavy objects, the VC were everywhere all at once like spider cancer, and instead of losing the war in little pieces over the years we lost it fast in under a week. After that ... we were dead but too dumb to lie down."

North Vietnam's General Giap made a similar assessment:

"Until Tet they [the Americans] thought they could win the war, but now they knew they could not."

CHANGING ATTITUDES

The Tet offensive brought about a major change in U.S. policy towards the Vietnam conflict. Before the Tet offensive, General Westmoreland had been granted all of his demands for more troops. Now, however, his requests were met with skepticism.

While President Johnson sat in the Oval Office, he could often hear antiwar protesters gathered outside the White House as they chanted, "Hey, hey, LBJ, how many kids have you killed today?" Johnson was bitterly angry over the protests, but the Tet offensive had nonetheless left the president and his policy advisers in a terrible quandary. If more men, more money, and more equipment could not win the war in Vietnam, what would?

JOHNSON'S ANNOUNCEMENT

On March 31, 1968, Lyndon Johnson shocked his supporters by announcing that he would not run for re-election. During Johnson's presidency, South Vietnam had been prevented from falling to communism, and an escalation of the war that could have entangled China or the Soviet Union had also been avoided. Now, however, Johnson believed that there was nothing more he could do in Vietnam.

NUMBER OF U.S. TROOPS IN VIETNAM	
1960	900
1962	11,000
1965	(June) 50,000
1965	(December) 180,000
1967	389,000
1969	540,000
1970	335,000
1971	160,000
1973	160

ANTIWAR PROTESTS

As U.S. involvement in the Vietnam conflict steadily deepened and the draft continued, demonstrations against the war also increased.

Young protesters were often dismissed by many older Americans for being part of a "hippy" counterculture that rejected traditional American values and embraced experimentation with sex and drugs. Yet the protests represented a genuine, and growing, resistance in the United States to the country's role in the Vietnam conflict.

Antiwar demonstrations, which reached their peak with a march of 500,000 people on Washington in November 1969, sent a message to both U.S. and North Vietnamese leaders. In the United States, they were a clear indication that massive casualties in Vietnam would not be acceptable to the American people. The protests also revealed to North Vietnam that its enemy did not have unconditional support at home.

A great number of more conservative Americans, however, supported U.S. involvement in Vietnam. For these people, the antiwar demonstrations stirred a deep resentment.

▼ Waving a variety of flags, including that of communist North Vietnam, demonstrators in New York City march in protest against U.S. involvement in Vietnam.

Peace with Honor, 1968–1970

"THE WILL TO WIN"

During the 1968 presidential election campaign, Republican candidate Richard M. Nixon offered the American people an alternative to Johnson's Vietnam policy. Nixon had actually set out the basis for this policy in an article he wrote for *Reader's Digest* in 1964. Believing that a communist victory in South Vietnam would be a catastrophe, Nixon advocated making full use of U.S. military might. "All that is needed," he wrote, "is the will to win — and the courage to use our power."

Nixon won the 1968 presidential election in part because his proposals for Vietnam appealed to a broad base of voters. If many Americans opposed U.S. involvement in Vietnam, many others believed that U.S. troops should stay in the country and stop the spread of communism — and they also believed that the antiwar demonstrations were part of a larger

▼ Richard Nixon on the campaign trail in 1968. Vice president under Eisenhower and the Republican nominee for president in 1960, Nixon was already a familiar public figure. He promised to end the war in Vietnam without sacrificing U.S. dignity.

erosion of American values. In a reference to the noisy antiwar demonstrations, Nixon called these conservative voters the "silent majority." During the election campaign he promised them he would "end the war and win the peace."

"VIETNAMIZATION"

Nixon's strategy for Vietnam, which he called "peace with honor," was based on a policy known as "Vietnamization" that was first initiated by President Johnson. Vietnamization involved offering military equipment and training to the South Vietnamese forces so they could fight the communists on their own. U.S. soldiers would stay in Vietnam while the South Vietnamese forces were built up and improved, but their numbers would be gradually reduced.

RICHARD NIXON (1913–1994)

Former vice president of the United States and John Kennedy's Republican opponent in the 1960 presidential election, Richard Nixon was a man who inspired strong opinions. Some admired his tough anti-communist stance, while others thought him a cynical, underhanded opportunist.

As a politician, Nixon took full advantage of Cold War hysteria and was a prominent supporter of Senator Joseph McCarthy and his communist witch-hunts in the 1950s. He once confided to a friend, "if you can't lie, you'll never go anywhere." Ironically, Nixon presided over the warming of relations between the United States and both China and the Soviet Union. Nixon resigned the presidency following the Watergate scandal.

DEFENDING THE FREE WORLD

Once South Vietnam could fend for itself, Nixon argued, the United States could withdraw from the conflict without the disgrace of defeat. Like most U.S. leaders of the Cold War era, Nixon believed that the United States had to maintain its credibility as champion of the "free," or non-communist, world. According to the Cold War thinking of the day, the United States could not back down from defending a nation against communist aggressors, because doing so would invite communist powers like the Soviet Union and China to spread their influence to other parts of the world.

President Nixon was determined to use all of the United States' military strength to achieve his aims. One of his first and most important appointments was that of Henry Kissinger as U.S. national security adviser. The two men began to plot the course of U.S. policy in Vietnam.

HENRY KISSINGER (1923–)

A Jewish refugee from Nazi Germany, the brilliant, intensely ambitious Kissinger proved to be as ruthless and cunning as Nixon when it came to foreign affairs. In 1973 Nixon appointed Kissinger secretary of state, a post he continued to hold under President Gerald Ford. Explaining his attitude towards international politics, Kissinger had this to say:

"The superpowers often behave like two heavily armed blind men feeling their way around a room, each believing himself in mortal peril from the other, whom he assumes to have perfect vision ... Of course, even two blind men can do enormous damage to each other, not to speak of the room."

CAMBODIA BOMBED

Nixon and Kissinger adopted the North Vietnamese tactic of both fighting and negotiating. While pressing for results with the North Vietnamese at the Paris Peace Talks, which had dragged on since May 1968, Nixon ordered a bombing campaign on Cambodia in March 1969. Cambodia borders Vietnam, and the North Vietnamese had long crossed the border to use the country's dense jungle as a base for attacks on South Vietnam.

Nixon kept the bombing secret from the public. He believed news of the bombing would provoke demonstrations, which in turn would lead the North Vietnamese to conclude that the American people did not support him.

"MADMAN THEORY"

The president also played up his anticommunist reputation. He threatened the North Vietnamese with "measures of great consequence and force" if they refused to negotiate with him, making a thinly veiled reference to the United States' huge nuclear arsenal. Nixon never intended to use these weapons. "I call it the madman theory," he confided to a presidential aide. "I want the North Vietnamese to believe I'll do anything to stop the war. We'll slip the word to them that 'for God's sake, you know Nixon is obsessed about communists. We can't restrain him when he's angry — and he has his hand on the nuclear button' — and Ho Chi Minh himself will be in Paris in two days begging for peace."

Nixon and his advisers did have some reason to be optimistic about Vietnam in early 1969. Although the prestige of the

U.S. military had suffered from the severe pounding of the Tet offensive, and the American people were divided over their support for the war, the situation in Vietnam wasn't as bad as it might have seemed. The Tet offensive was, after all, a communist defeat. North Vietnam had played its best shot, and when the dust settled the South Vietnamese regime and their U.S. allies were still standing.

COLD WAR POLITICS

In addition, important shifts were occurring in world politics, shifts that Nixon hoped to turn to his advantage. China and the Soviet Union may have both been communist regimes, but they still had significant political differences. During the 1960s, relations between them grew frostier, and a border dispute in 1969 actually resulted in fighting between Soviet and Chinese troops. The increased hostility between the Soviet Union and China encouraged each country to seek better relations with the United States.

Throughout the Vietnam War, the Soviet Union had been North Vietnam's staunchest supporter, but now the Soviets were losing enthusiasm. Originally, the Soviets had supported North Vietnam simply because it was fighting against a U.S.-backed ally and U.S. troops. The Soviets, however, had sent a great deal of aid to Vietnam that they could not really afford to give, and as the war dragged on Soviet leaders concluded that goods sent to Vietnam could be put to better use in their own country. In short, the Soviets were as eager for the Vietnam conflict to end as the United States. Like the United States, however, they did not want to abandon an ally and thus appear weak to their Cold War enemies.

▼ Suspected of being communist guerillas, these bound and blindfolded men wait for interrogation by U.S. soldiers.

LE DUAN TAKES OVER

Despite Nixon's hints of nuclear catastrophe, Ho Chi Minh did not rush to Paris to beg for peace, for the simple reason that he was too ill. His health began to fail in early 1969, and though he worked until August of that year, he died on September 2, 1969, at the age of seventy-nine.

The death of Ho Chi Minh inspired hope among U.S. officials that North Vietnam might take a softer line towards the conflict, but Ho's successor, Le Duan, was also unbending as a leader. Under Le Duan, the North Vietnamese still had one clear objective — the unification of Vietnam under their communist regime. Neither U.S. bombing threats nor pressure from the Soviets to compromise seemed to have any effect on their determination to achieve this objective.

FLAWS OF VIETNAMIZATION

Vietnamization, meanwhile, was proving difficult to implement. Nixon had spelled out the policy to President Thieu in June 1969. Like most other South Vietnamese politicians, Thieu was suspicious, since he saw the policy as a way for the United States to withdraw from the war. Yet even if President Thieu had been enthusiastic about the policy, it still had a fatal flaw — the awful condition of the South Vietnamese army. Most of its officers were alarmingly corrupt and incompetent. For example, many officers exaggerated the number of men under their command in order to receive more pay. During the entire conflict, South Vietnamese soldiers had been consistently reluctant to fight. Most were happy to let U.S. soldiers fight the communists for them.

During the course of a year, one in ten South Vietnamese soldiers deserted, and Vietnamization only increased the problem. Sometimes deserters would

RESENTFUL TROOPS

Though meant to take pressure off of U.S. troops, Vietnamization only stirred up more resentment among them. As GI Thomas Kingsley tells a friend:

" ... there's a bitter hatred between us and the South Vietnam troops because they carry new weapons and we don't; and we do all the goddamn fighting while they sit on their asses all the time. Man, it makes you burn."

Broadcast journalist Edward R. Murrow said:

"Anyone who isn't confused doesn't really understand the situation."

hide their uniforms and pretend to be communist guerrillas to take advantage of South Vietnam's "open arms" policy, which offered money and other incentives to rebels who surrendered.

TROOPS RETURN

Nixon did enjoy less opposition to the war at home. The troop withdrawals he ordered had a noticeable impact on antiwar demonstrations, which, though they continued, became less attended as more soldiers returned. The Nixon administration also launched ferocious attacks on antiwar protesters. Playing on class differences — many demonstrators were middle-class college students, while the war's strongest supporters often came from the working class — Vice President Spiro Agnew called the protesters "an effete corps of impudent snobs".

▼ Weary U.S. troops march out of their base at Quang Tri on the first step of their return home. U.S. troop numbers in Vietnam declined rapidly after Nixon became president.

U.S. OPTIMISM

Like Kennedy and Johnson before him, Nixon believed that the United States' wealth, technological superiority, and military power could win the conflict in Vietnam. During the summer of 1969, the United States put men on the Moon. If the United States could do that, then surely it could triumph over a tiny little country in Southeast Asia.

MY LAI MASSACRE

One sign that Nixon's optimism was resting on shaky ground came in early 1969, with an incident in South Vietnam that would have a profound effect on the American public's perception of the war. On March 16, a group of U.S. soldiers under the command of Lieutenant William Calley gathered several hundred men, women, and children from the village of My Lai and murdered them.

If massacres like the one at My Lai were not everyday occurrences in Vietnam, they were also not isolated events. My Lai came to symbolize the attitude of many U.S. soldiers towards the people they were supposed to be protecting. Historian Loren Baritz evokes the image of "nineteen-year-old Americans, brought up on World War II movies and Westerns, walking through the jungle, armed to the teeth, searching for an invisible enemy …" Many of these young

▶ Even the presence of a photographer did not prevent this U.S. soldier from hitting a disarmed Vietcong prisoner. This kind of violence was often prompted by the frustration U.S. soldiers felt at being attacked by an invisible enemy who could strike at any time and then vanish into the jungle.

As a "med-vac" (medical evacuation) helicopter hovers in the background, U.S. soldiers sift through the grisly remains of a Vietcong ambush. The communist rebels favored this kind of tactic, which allowed them to attack U.S. forces only when the situation was to their advantage.

men found the peasant lifestyle and Buddhist customs of the rural Vietnamese baffling. They referred to them with such racist terms as "dinks," "slopes," and "gooks."

As members of their platoon were picked off one by one by booby traps, sniper fire, or hit-and-run ambushes by an enemy they almost never saw, many U.S. soldiers came to regard all Vietnamese as the enemy.

When the facts about the My Lai massacre emerged a year or so after it took place, antiwar protesters were not the only ones outraged. Many Americans who supported the war were shocked to hear of their own forces behaving with the same callous brutality as the Nazi and Japanese soldiers of World War II.

A GI'S BITTERNESS

This is a war of the Unwilling
Led by the Unqualified
Dying for the Ungrateful

GRAFFITI IN GI LAVATORY, SAIGON

CHAPTER SEVEN

The War Spreads, 1970–1973

CAMBODIA AND LAOS

Beginning in 1970, the war in Vietnam spread to other parts of Southeast Asia. Two countries on the western border of Vietnam — Cambodia and Laos — were each drawn into the conflict. Cambodia was the first to experience fighting.

While the Cambodian government of Prince Sihanouk was anticommunist, Sihanouk opposed U.S. involvement in Vietnam and cut diplomatic relations with the United States because of it. Sihanouk had allowed the Ho Chi Minh Trail to pass through his country, in exchange for North Vietnam's agreement not to support a group of communist guerillas in Cambodia known as the Khmer Rouge. This arrangement worked well for Sihanouk until the North Vietnamese presence in Cambodia and the Khmer Rouge threat became too strong to ignore.

Sihanouk described his country as being "caught between the hammer and the anvil." In March 1970, he was ousted from power and replaced by Lon Nol, a pro-U.S. general who disapproved of the North Vietnamese being in Cambodia.

INVASION OF CAMBODIA

One of Nixon's first decisions as president had been to bomb North Vietnamese bases in Cambodia. Now, with a pro-U.S. regime in control of the country, he authorized an all-out ground attack. On April 30, 1970, South Vietnamese and U.S. troops numbering 80,000 strong poured into Cambodia to seek out and

▼ Vietnam, Laos, and Cambodia had once been united as the French colony of Indochina. The Mekong River links them all, and they are each cloaked in thick tropical vegetation.

destroy North Vietnamese bases. Their main target was the Central Office for South Vietnam (COSVN), which was North Vietnam's military headquarters in Cambodia. When the troops arrived, however, they found a few deserted huts — the North Vietnamese had vanished into the jungle. After the U.S. and ARVN troops left, the communists returned. Once again, North Vietnam's low-tech approach to war had trumped U.S. might.

The invasion had catastrophic consequences for Cambodia. North Vietnam began aiding the Khmer Rouge, whom they had previously ignored. Fighting between the Khmer Rouge and Lon Nol's government escalated into full-scale civil war and led to an eventual communist victory.

The political fallout for Nixon, while minor in comparison, was still significant. Many Americans were deeply unhappy about the spread of a conflict that was supposed to be ending. The invasion sparked more protests. During demonstrations at Kent State University in Ohio, four student protesters were shot dead by members of the National Guard, causing further outrage.

▲ This photograph, which appeared on the front page of newspapers around the world, shows the anguish and outrage of a student demonstrator at Kent State University in Ohio. She is kneeling by the body of one of four students shot dead during antiwar protests.

LAOS IN THE FIRING LINE

Nine months later, the presence of the North Vietnamese in Laos also provoked an invasion. On January 30, 1971, South Vietnamese troops, heavily supported by U.S. aircraft and artillery positions, attacked North Vietnamese forces in Laos. Although the planes and artillery inflicted losses, the South Vietnamese troops fought badly against North Vietnam's forces. After the initial attack, they fled in chaos.

President Nixon during his historic visit to China in 1972. Here he walks along the Great Wall with Chinese premier Zhou En Lai.

DÉTENTE?

Opposition in the United States to its involvement in Vietnam was good news for North Vietnamese leaders. Since 1968 they had been rebuilding their forces for another great offensive, but as the 70s wore on it seemed that time was running out. While the North Vietnamese had hung on against the immense power of the United States, the conflict was taking its toll on the commitment of North Vietnam's Soviet and Chinese supporters.

During the early 1970s, the talk in international politics was of détente, a French word that means "relaxation." After two decades of outright hostility, the United States, Soviet Union, and China all concluded that the world would be a safer place if relations between them improved. To move the process along, President Nixon visited the Soviet Union and, in a historic first for a U.S. president, also visited communist China. During most of the 1970s, the Cold War became a little less frosty.

For the leaders of both North and South Vietnam, détente was not a welcome development. Their countries had each been supported by the Cold War's rival superpowers. As the conflict dragged on, however, they sensed that their powerful allies were losing interest.

THE EASTER OFFENSIVE

The North Vietnamese finally attacked South Vietnam on March 30, 1972, in what came to be known as the Easter offensive. Troops swarmed in from bases in North Vietnam and Cambodia, joining Vietcong guerillas to strike at various positions in South Vietnam. The communists assumed that South Vietnamese forces would collapse when attacked, just like they did in Laos. At first, the South Vietnamese did crumble, and the communist offensive went extremely well.

Like the South Vietnamese troops, U.S. forces were caught by surprise, but they recovered quickly. Nixon immediately authorized massive air attacks against military targets in North Vietnam. U.S. Navy ships off the coast of Vietnam blockaded the country, and mines were placed in North Vietnam's main harbor, Haiphong. With U.S. air and artillery support, the South Vietnamese army then launched a massive and successful counterattack.

The Easter offensive was ultimately a disaster for North Vietnam. While South Vietnam suffered 25,000 deaths in the fighting, North Vietnam lost 100,000 men — and President Thieu was still in power in Saigon. Although North Vietnam's Chinese and Soviet allies made strong public protests against the U.S. bombing, privately they urged North Vietnam to negotiate with the United States to bring the war to an end.

PARIS PEACE TALKS

While the Paris Peace Talks had dragged on since 1968, they now began to achieve some results. In October 1972, Henry Kissinger and Le Duc Tho, North Vietnam's principal negotiator, announced they had reached a settlement that both found acceptable.

Kissinger, however, had not consulted the South Vietnamese when reaching this settlement. Although they took part in the Paris Peace Talks, they had no interest in the United States withdrawing from the conflict in Vietnam, and their lack of cooperation during the talks had seriously hindered any progress. When Kissinger brought the agreement to Thieu, he rejected it angrily. The North Vietnamese, in turn, were suspicious of Thieu's rejection, which they saw as a ploy. The talks foundered.

THE PARIS AGREEMENT

The settlement made by Kissinger and Le Duc Tho contained the following points:

- There would be an immediate cease-fire.

- Armies from both sides would keep control of whatever territory they held at the time of the cease-fire.

- U.S. troops would leave Vietnam within sixty days.

- Prisoners of war would be exchanged.

- After the cease-fire, a political settlement would be negotiated that would include democratic elections and the reunification of Vietnam.

PEACE BREAKS DOWN

In December 1972, President Nixon ordered further air strikes against North Vietnam. The strikes went on for eleven days and were the most intense bombing attacks of the war. They caused a huge outcry, not only from North Vietnam's communist allies and American antiwar protesters, but also from U.S. allies in Europe.

The attacks were carried out partly to encourage North Vietnam to make more concessions at the peace talks and partly to reassure President Thieu that the United States was not deserting South Vietnam. The United States also provided massive military aid to strengthen the South Vietnamese army.

▶ Flanked by diplomats from their respective countries, Henry Kissinger (top) and Le Duc Tho (bottom) square off against each other with steely, poker-faced determination at the Paris Peace Talks.

PEACE WITH HONOR?

Peace talks began again in January 1973. After the United States threatened to sign a treaty without South Vietnam, Thieu reluctantly agreed to a set of conditions very similar to those negotiated by Henry Kissinger and Le Duc Tho in 1972.

On January 27, 1973, North Vietnam, South Vietnam, and the United States signed a settlement known as the "Paris Agreement." True to the agreement, the last U.S. combat troops left South Vietnam on March 29, 1973.

When President Nixon announced the breakthrough, he claimed that "we have finally achieved peace with honor." Nixon's statement, however, was simply not true. The United States had spent billions of dollars and sacrificed thousands of lives to support South Vietnam. The country, however, was no better able to defend itself against its communist opponents than it had been in 1963.

AMERICAN MORALE

Even in the early 1970s, many U.S. policy advisers still considered the United States' struggle against communism in Vietnam to be of vital importance:

"The future of Western civilization is at stake in the way you handle yourselves in Vietnam."

SIR ROBERT THOMPSON, BRITISH GUERRILLA WARFARE SPECIALIST, TO RICHARD NIXON, 1971

At the same time, however, many U.S. soldiers felt they were fighting a war they could neither believe in nor win, and the morale of U.S. troops in Vietnam plummeted. Black and Latino soldiers in particular felt they had been singled out to do the worst of the fighting. Some soldiers began to paint peace signs and antiwar slogans on their uniforms. Officers often had to argue with men who refused to obey orders during combat. Drug use increased to the point where it became commonplace. Unpopular officers were sometimes killed by their own men, often by a fragmentation grenade rolled into their tent at night — a practice known as "fragging."

"No Vietcong ever called me nigger."

BLACK GI SLOGAN

"The frank thing is, there just wasn't a hell of a lot worth dying for."

LIEUTENANT BILL KENERLY

Many U.S. soldiers in Vietnam were not secretive about their opposition to the war. These soldiers are giving the "V" peace sign, popularized by such antiwar celebrities as John Lennon. A "ban the bomb" flag also flies over their heads.

CHAPTER EIGHT

Final Conflict, 1973–1975

A FRAGILE PEACE

With the United States gone, Thieu's government held out against the communists for two years, one month, and a day. In a sense, it is surprising the regime lasted that long.

No one seriously expected the Paris Agreement to end the war in Vietnam. When the cease-fire was declared, North and South Vietnam were as hostile to each other as ever, and many observers expected an eventual victory by North Vietnam. At the time, however, neither side was in a position of strength.

North Vietnam used the 1973 cease-fire to recover from the devastating losses of the Easter offensive. In June of that year the North Vietnamese leader, Le Duan, visited both his communist allies, China and the Soviet Union. He hoped to persuade them to supply more aid for a final offensive, but neither of the two communist superpowers showed much interest. In the era of détente, both were far more concerned with improving relations with the United States.

▼ As the conflict in Vietnam came to a close, North Vietnam released U.S. prisoners of war, almost all of whom were pilots and other aircrew. These U.S. prisoners, photographed in Hanoi in March 1973, begin their journey home.

Yet although both North and South Vietnam had lost the full-scale support of their powerful allies, the effect was far less devastating to North Vietnam. After all, no Chinese or Soviet troops had fought in Vietnam, while the South Vietnamese had relied heavily upon U.S. troops.

Theoretically, South Vietnam at least had a fighting chance. The U.S. presence was slim but not nonexistent. In addition to a detachment of 159 marines to guard the U.S. embassy, as well as 10,000 U.S. civilians who were mostly connected to the military, the United States had left behind its military bases and billions of dollars worth of equipment. Nixon had promised Thieu that the United States would not desert him, and he had threatened North Vietnam with dire consequences should it break the cease-fire. Thieu had an army that was now a million strong and equipped with the best military technology available. Yet in the end, the weaknesses of the South Vietnamese armed forces could not be overcome.

A NORTH VIETNAMESE PERSPECTIVE

"Our troops were exhausted and their units in disarray. We had not been able to make up our losses. We were short of manpower as well as food and ammunition, and coping with the enemy was very difficult."

NORTH VIETNAMESE GENERAL TRAN VAN TRA, ON THE CONDITION OF HIS MEN FIGHTING IN THE SOUTH IN 1973

AT WAR AGAIN

The cease-fire soon broke down, and at first the South Vietnamese forces performed surprisingly well. Much of the territory lost to the communists before the Paris Agreement was recovered. Yet the North Vietnamese held on, reverting to low-key guerilla tactics while they regained their strength and waited. They could afford to bide their time. In 1973 they were the third largest army in the world.

Despite all its advantages, Thieu's regime was doomed. Ultimately, South Vietnam could simply not establish itself as a strong and viable nation. The government in Saigon had never managed to gain any widespread support from the civilian population of South Vietnam. Thieu's primary strength came from South Vietnam's armed forces, but even its members were divided in their support.

AN ARMY IN DISARRAY

South Vietnam's fighting forces were hopelessly corrupt and incompetent. They were led by commanders who paid so little that the soldiers had to steal food to survive. U.S. officers knew that if the troops they were commanding were pinned down by enemy fire, they could radio for air support. Within minutes, U.S. planes would scream over the horizon to rain down bullets and missiles on the enemy. South Vietnamese soldiers, meanwhile, had to bribe the Air Force to fly missions to support them.

Worse was to come for South Vietnam. U.S. aid still continued, but the sophisticated U.S. weapons that had been left behind required fuel and spare parts that the South Vietnamese could neither find nor afford. The country's economy, already reeling from the loss of 300,000 jobs that the U.S. military presence had provided, also suffered from both a poor rice harvest and a global fuel crisis brought on by massive increases in the price of oil.

CASUALTY FIGURES

These casualty figures for the Vietnam conflict cover the period from 1954 to 1975. While their accuracy cannot be guaranteed, the figures are broadly accepted by historians.

NORTH VIETNAM

1,100,000 soldiers killed

600,000 soldiers wounded

26,000 soldiers captured

2,000,000 civilians killed

SOUTH VIETNAM

223,748 soldiers killed

1,169,763 soldiers wounded

415,000 civilians killed

UNITED STATES

58,219 soldiers killed

304,704 soldiers wounded

766 soldiers captured

THE WORLD TURNS ITS BACK

By October 1973, barely nine months after the cease-fire had been declared, full-scale war was raging in Vietnam. Yet the rest of the world was not particularly interested. Most war correspondents and photographers were engrossed with events in the Middle East, where another U.S. ally, Israel, was fighting for survival against its hostile Arab neighbors.

Nixon, meanwhile, was sinking fast, his presidency now fatally tarnished by the Watergate scandal, which involved the break-in of Democratic headquarters by Republican operatives during the 1972 presidential campaign and a subsequent cover-up that reached to the top of his administration. Nixon resigned in August 1974 and was replaced by Vice President Gerald Ford. Although Ford reassured South Vietnam that he would continue U.S. support, he had no good reason to do so.

NORTH VIETNAM'S LAST OFFENSIVE

By the end of 1974, the North Vietnamese felt strong enough to attempt another offensive. As they had before, they hoped that an attack on South Vietnam would trigger an uprising against Thieu's regime. They decided to move cautiously. Still unsure of U.S. intentions, they feared another massive bombing campaign.

In December 1974, North Vietnamese forces attacked and quickly overran the central highlands province of Phuoc Long. The United States did not react, and more attacks in early 1975 brought further advances. Thieu then ordered his army to retreat and form a defensive line just north of Saigon, but the retreat turned into a chaotic rout. Fearing defeat, thousands of South Vietnamese soldiers deserted, and a half million refugees poured into Saigon.

President Thieu resigned on April 21, 1975. In his farewell speech, he promised to "stand shoulder to shoulder with the compatriots and combatants to defend the country." Instead, Thieu fled to Taiwan.

▼ South Vietnamese refugees, desperate to flee from the approaching North Vietnamese forces, board a cargo ship at Da Nang in 1975.

Fear of execution by communist soldiers made escape a matter of life or death for many South Vietnamese. Here at Nha Trang in April 1975, a U.S. official punches a man away from an aircraft that is already dangerously overloaded with refugees.

THE LAST BATTLE

In her book *Novel Without a Name*, North Vietnamese novelist Duong Thu Huong describes the final battle for Saigon:

"The battle unfolded as predictably as if it had been a parade: assault, a rapid conclusion. Compared to the battles of the last ten years, it almost seemed like a game …"

SAIGON FALLS

North Vietnamese troops reached Saigon so quickly that the United States had to airlift 900 of its own people, as well as 5,000 Vietnamese, out of the capital to aircraft carriers waiting off the coast. Television news programs showed unforgettable footage of terrified Vietnamese officials, certain they would be executed if they stayed behind, fighting desperately to get aboard an evacuation helicopter. Out at sea, aircraft carrier flight decks became so crowded that many idle helicopters were pushed into the water to make way for those coming in. This waste of expensive technology seemed a fitting symbol of the U.S. involvement in the war. U.S. ships were also besieged by South Vietnamese fleeing by boat. One aircraft carrier took on an extraordinary 10,000 refugees.

In Saigon, television crews filmed a North Vietnamese T-54 tank battering down the iron fence of the presidential palace. Other tanks followed behind. Bounding from the leading tank was Colonel Bui Tin, who entered the palace to take the South Vietnamese surrender.

Waiting for him was Thieu's replacement, General Duang Van Minh. He greeted Bui Tin with these words: "I have been waiting since early this morning to transfer power to you." Bui Tin was brusque and brutally honest. "There's no question of you transferring power," he said. "Your power has crumbled. You cannot give up what you do not have."

The city of Saigon fell with little fighting. After thirty years and over three million deaths, the Vietnam War had finally ground to a halt.

▼ A North Vietnamese tank crashes through the fence of Saigon's presidential palace on April 30, 1975. The fall of Saigon marked the end of thirty years of fighting in Vietnam.

Consequences of the War, 1976 to Present

LE DUAN'S TRIUMPH

On May 15, 1975, Vietnamese leader Le Duan delivered these triumphant words during celebrations in Hanoi to mark the communist victory: "We hail the new era … of brilliant prospects for the development of a peaceful, independent, reunified, democratic, prosperous, and strong Vietnam."

Even today, however, those brilliant prospects have yet to be realized. The story of Vietnam in peace is almost as tragic as that of Vietnam at war.

▼ U.S. and South Vietnamese officials on the roof of the U.S. embassy in Saigon, just before the city falls. They await a fleet of helicopters to ferry them to U.S. aircraft carriers and safety.

RE-EDUCATION

When the North Vietnamese arrived in Saigon, many South Vietnamese government and military officials who had not managed to escape feared for their lives. After all, government officials had been killed by the thousands in Hue when that city was occupied by the North Vietnamese during the Tet offensive. Yet the expected massacre did not take place. Instead, South Vietnamese officials were sent to "re-education camps," where they were force-fed communist teachings and asked to repent their former lives. Such an experience might have been unpleasant, but far worse could have occurred.

THE DOMINOES FALL

Far worse did occur in Cambodia and Laos. Ironically, U.S. military action in these two countries actually increased communist opposition, thus helping to bring about the spread of communism that the United States sought to stop with its domino theory foreign policy. As the Vietnam war ended, both Cambodia and Laos fell to communist regimes. In Laos, the Pathet Lao party murdered 100,000 pro-U.S. Hmong guerrilla fighters.

"YEAR ZERO" IN CAMBODIA

When the Khmer Rouge took over Cambodia, they called for a complete social revolution. Declaring 1975 to be "Year Zero," they began systematically eliminating anyone they suspected of being "bourgeois," or middle class. For this fanatical regime, even owning a pair of glasses or having soft hands was evidence enough to warrant execution. At least a million Cambodians died in what became known as "the killing fields" before the regime fell in December 1978.

CHAOS IN SOUTHEAST ASIA

The worst atrocities occured in Cambodia. The communist Khmer Rouge captured the capital of Phnom Penh on April 17, 1975 — two weeks before the fall of Saigon. Led by a despotic communist named Pol Pot, the Khmer Rouge emptied Cambodia's cities and forced their inhabitants to work in agricultural communes. After nearly four years and the deaths of over a million Cambodians, an invasion by Vietnam toppled Pol Pot's vicious regime.

Vietnam's intervention in December 1978, which was brought about in part by border conflicts with the Khmer Rouge, in turn provoked a brief invasion of North Vietnam by China, who supported the Khmer Rouge. The result was the persecution in Vietnam of Vietnamese of Chinese origin.

▼ These piles of skulls at a Cambodian village are grisly reminders of the atrocities inflicted on Cambodia by the Khmer Rouge.

THE LEGACY OF WAR

Physically, Vietnam was left in a devastated condition by the war. The bombing campaigns had left huge craters across the country and had also destroyed most industrial sites and transportation systems. Defoliant chemicals sprayed by U.S. planes had polluted and destroyed much of Vietnam's fertile land, and many of the peasants who had been driven from their fields during the war were reluctant to return. The result was near starvation. Mines, as well as unexploded bombs and shells, also littered the country, and in the coming years their victims would often be women and children.

The United States had spent $167 billion on Vietnam during the war, while China and the Soviet Union also spent undisclosed but vast amounts of money. Now the war was over and the world's superpowers had cut off their spending. Once Vietnam had its falling out with China over the Cambodian invasion, it could count only the Soviet Union as an ally. Unfortunately, in the late 70s and early 80s the Soviet Union had little aid to spare for Vietnam, since its own economy was doing so poorly.

▼ This 1972 photograph shows the devastated city of Quang Tri. For Vietnam, recovery from the war's destruction would take many decades.

THE "BOAT PEOPLE"

Vietnam became one of the poorest countries in the world, and as its problems mounted, many Vietnamese decided to flee the country. If they paid the government a fee they were allowed to leave on dangerously overcrowded boats, where they would be at the mercy of storms, pirates, and any foreign government that would have them. Over 1.5 million "boat people" left Vietnam, and most ended up in refugee camps in Hong Kong, Thailand, and Malaysia. This spectacle was a deeply shameful one for Vietnam. Many refugees were sent home by neighboring countries unable to cope with such a huge influx of people. The one million Vietnamese who settled in the United States became another legacy of the war.

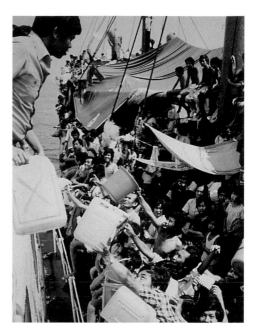

▲ Vietnamese "boat people," stranded in the Philippines for ten weeks in 1979, beg passing ships for water.

"CHILDREN OF THE DUST"

The war left behind another tragedy. Thousands of children had been born to Vietnamese women and U.S. soldiers. These children, who were either unknown to their American fathers or abandoned by them, were called "children of the dust" in postwar Vietnam. Despised and rejected by the other Vietnamese, they usually had to beg to stay alive.

VIETNAM VETERANS

U.S. soldiers returning from Vietnam often faced hostility from their fellow citizens. Many veterans, feeling shunned and isolated, turned to drugs and alcohol to wipe out the nightmare of Vietnam. Divorce, unemployment, and crime rates for Vietnam veterans are all higher than those of the general population.

CHANGE BEYOND RECOGNITION

U.S. soldiers called their country "the World." When they returned, however, they found that many things were bewilderingly different.

"I didn't come home; I just came back. Home had changed so much that I didn't recognize it. And no one recognized me either."

ANONYMOUS GI, QUOTED IN JOHN CLARK PRATT'S *VIETNAM VOICES*

"I managed to survive Vietnam and got back to New York … The change was just shocking. Clothes had changed. People's attitudes had changed. Close friends … that had been clean-cut, athletic types … now had hair down to their shoulders. They were wearin' … beards and bell-bottom pants … an' givin' peace signs. And I think I, like a lot of other guys, just kind of withdrew."

CORPORAL VITO J. LAVACCA

DISILLUSIONMENT

The Vietnam war had a profound impact on the American people's perception of their government and its policies. The antiwar demonstrations that often provoked violent clashes between police and protesters were actually symptoms of a much larger trend that would take hold after the war. Simply put, the fact that the U.S. government consistently lied about and concealed its actions in Vietnam helped lead to widespread disillusionment with government and a general loss of respect for authority. Black soldiers, in particular, believed they had been unfairly singled out to do the fighting in Vietnam, and this conviction contributed to the growing divide between the black community and mainstream white America.

Beyond its impact at home, the Vietnam conflict also exerted a tremendous influence on U.S. foreign policy. After Vietnam, the United States hesitated to commit ground troops to conflicts that could not be quickly and decisively won. In the 1980s, communist uprisings in the Central American countries of Nicaragua and El Salvador were dealt with in a clandestine manner meant to avoid arousing public opposition, with secret U.S. funding and training of the anticommunist opposition but no direct involvement in the conflicts. The United States only committed troops to battle if it was sure of victory — such as in 1983, when U.S. forces invaded the tiny Caribbean island of Grenada, which had been taken over by a communist regime.

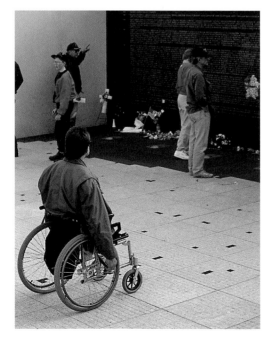

▼ U.S. soldiers returned from Vietnam to find their sacrifices were largely unappreciated, but since the war many memorials have been built to honor those who died in Vietnam. Here a wheelchair-bound veteran visits a memorial in St. Paul, Minnesota.

DIFFERING NEWS

In the decades following the war, historians have argued over why the U.S. intervention in Vietnam was such a disaster. Some historians support the view of General Westmoreland, who believed that the United States lost the war because the civilian government, influenced by the antiwar protesters and an unsympathetic media, severely limited the role of the armed forces. Westmoreland believed he could have won if he had been allowed to make full use of U.S. military power and wage a full-scale conflict.

Others historians think this view is too simplistic. They believe U.S. involvement failed because the South Vietnamese regime was simply too unstable. They argue that the United States relied too much on its technological superiority, and did not truly understand the unique circumstances of Vietnam.

OPPOSING ATTITUDES

Two statements reveal the attitudes of North Vietnam and the United States, and explain why one side triumphed and the other failed:

"If we must fight, we will fight. You can kill ten of my men for every one I kill of yours. But even at those odds, you will lose and I will win."

HO CHI MINH IN 1946, TO THE FRENCH PRIME MINISTER, AT THE START OF THE CONFLICT

"I can't believe that a fourth-rate power like North Vietnam doesn't have a breaking point."

HENRY KISSINGER IN 1969, WHILE TRYING TO FORCE THE NORTH VIETNAMESE TO MAKE CONCESSIONS AT THE PARIS PEACE TALKS

PEACE IN VIETNAM

While the Vietnam of today is still a very poor country, peace has finally arrived. The United States recognized the country's communist government in 1995, and since then Vietnam has improved relations with Western nations. Such communist economic policies as collectivized farming have been dropped, and private enterprise is now encouraged. Tourism is a major industry. Ironically, along with the beautiful temples and lush scenery, visitors also come to see crashed bombers, burned-out tanks, and other lingering remnants of the war.

THE UNWINNABLE WAR

In the 1960s, Vice President Hubert Humphrey had privately said of Vietnam, "America is throwing lives and money down a corrupt rat hole." Yet his own president, Lyndon Johnson, had also asserted, "The battle against communism must be joined in Southeast Asia with strength and determination … or the United States, inevitably, must surrender the Pacific and take up our defenses on our own shores." Ultimately, this Cold War thinking led to a long and unwinnable war, whose terrible consequences would have a tremendous impact on both the United States and Southeast Asia for years to come.

Time Line

1861
French forces seize Saigon and take substantial control of Vietnam

1883
France begins colonial rule of Indochina (modern-day Vietnam, Laos, and Cambodia)

1890
Ho Chi Minh born (leaves Vietnam in 1911)

1924
Ho Chi Minh becomes full-time communist agent for Soviet Union

1949
Communists seize control of China

1950
JUNE
Korean War begins

French receive U.S. military aid for conflict in Vietnam

1954
MAY
French surrender at Dien Bien Phu
JULY
Peace conference at Geneva leads to signing of Geneva Accords

Vietnam divided, on a temporary basis, into communist North Vietnam and non-communist South Vietnam

DECEMBER
North Vietnam sends its first regular troops to South Vietnam

1964
Gulf of Tonkin resolution gives U.S. president the power to engage U.S. combat troops in Vietnam without a formal declaration of war

1965
FEBRUARY
U.S. tactical air strikes and strategic bombing begin in Vietnam
MARCH
First U.S. combat troops arrive in Vietnam

JULY
Johnson commits to full U.S. military presence in Vietnam

JUNE
U.S. troop withdrawal begins in Vietnam
SEPTEMBER
Ho Chi Minh dies

1970
Vietnam conflict spreads to Cambodia

1971
Vietnam conflict spreads to Laos

1972
FEBRUARY
Nixon visits China
MARCH/APRIL
North Vietnam launches Easter offensive
MAY
Nixon visits Soviet Union

1940
Japan occupies Indochina, allows French to continue to govern the colony

1941
Ho Chi Minh returns to Vietnam and organizes Vietminh, who fight against the Japanese and the French

1945
Ho Chi Minh declares independence of Vietnam, while the French continue to control country

1946
NOVEMBER
French warships bombard Haiphong
DECEMBER
Vietminh forces begin guerilla war against the French

1955
Ngo Dinh Diem elected president of South Vietnam

1957
Civil war breaks out in South Vietnam between government troops and communist guerrillas

1962
U.S. involvement in Vietnam increases

1963
NOVEMBER
Diem assassinated; President John F. Kennedy assassinated; Vice President Lyndon Johnson becomes U.S. president

1967
SEPTEMBER
Nguyen Van Thieu elected president of South Vietnam

OCTOBER
Demonstrations against U.S. involvement in Vietnam erupt across the United States

1968
JANUARY
North Vietnam launches Tet offensive
MAY
Peace negotiations over conflict in Vietnam begin in Paris

1969
JANUARY
Richard Nixon sworn in as U.S. president
MARCH
The My Lai massacre takes place

1973
JANUARY
Paris Peace Agreement allows United States to withdraw from Vietnam
MARCH
Last U.S. troops leave Vietnam

1974
South Vietnamese government launches offensive against communist guerrillas in South Vietnam

1975
JANUARY
North Vietnam begins final offensive against South Vietnam

APRIL
Khmer Rouge take control of Cambodia; city of Saigon falls to communist forces and Vietnam War ends

Glossary

ARVN: acronym for the Army of the Republic of Vietnam, South Vietnam's main fighting force during the war.

Buddhism: religion, founded in India in the fifth century B.C. by Siddhartha Gautama ("Buddha"), that is popular throughout Asia.

capitalism: ideology and economic system based on individual ownership of property and a free, competitive market that determines prices and wages.

Cold War: rivalry between the United States and the Soviet Union, as well as their respective allies, that lasted between 1945 and 1991.

colony: territory a country controls in order to exploit its resources.

communism: ideology that advocates government owning all property and controlling the economy in order to create a classless society, and which usually involves authoritarian rule.

containment: during the Cold War, U.S. foreign policy that sought to contain communism in one country in order to stop its spread to other countries.

détente: diplomatic term that describes a lessening of tensions between former enemies and a period of greater understanding between them.

DMZ: acronym for demilitarized zone, which during the conflict in Vietnam was a stretch of land that separated North and South Vietnam.

domino theory: during the Cold War, belief that if one country in a region fell under communist control, then other countries in that region would each fall in turn, like a row of dominos.

Geneva Accords: settlement reached in 1954 that established the temporary division of Vietnam into communist North Vietnam and non-communist South Vietnam.

guerrilla warfare: type of warfare that involves small, mobile groups of soldiers who employ hit-and-run tactics but do not engage the enemy directly.

herbicide: chemical that kills vegetation.

Ho Chi Minh Trail: route that brought arms and troops from North Vietnam to communist rebels in South Vietnam.

ideology: belief or way of thinking, as in a communist or capitalist ideology.

Khmer Rouge: name of communist opposition in Cambodia, which siezed control of the country in 1975.

napalm: jelly-like, gasoline-based substance that bursts into flames upon contact with air.

pacification: during the Vietnam War, a campaign in South Vietnam that sought to eliminate communist activity.

Paris Agreement: settlement reached in 1973 that ended the United States' military involvement in Vietnam.

regime: system of government, or a group of people who rule a country.

Tet offensive: major assault by North Vietnam on South Vietnam in 1968.

Vietcong (VC): name that the South Vietnamese and U.S. military forces used to refer to communist guerrillas fighting in South Vietnam.

Vietminh: coalition of resistance groups in Vietnam, originally organized by Ho Chi Minh during World War II to fight against the Japanese and the French, that later fought the French for the independence of Vietnam.

Vietnamization: U.S. initiative to make South Vietnamese armed forces more effective so that U.S. troops could be phased out of the conflict in Vietnam.

Books

A Bright and Shining Lie
Neil Sheehan (Vintage Books)

Dispatches
Michael Herr (Vintage Books)

Novel Without a Name
Duong Thu Huong (Penguin)

Vietnam: A History
Stanley Karnow (Penguin)

Vietnam Voices
John Clark Pratt
(University of Georgia Press)

The Vietnam War
(*Seminar Studies in History* series)
Mitchell Hall (Longman)

Videos

Archives of War: Volume Six, Vietnam
(MPI Home Video)

Guerilla Warfare: Vietnam
(U.S. News *Masters of War* series)
(Unapix)

Vietnam: A Television History
(WGBH Boston Video)

Vietnam: In the Year of the Pig
(MPI Home Video)

Vietnam: Ten Thousand Day War
(Ghadar and Associates)

The War at Home
(First Run Features)

Web Sites

Vets with a Mission
www.vwam.com

Vietnam Online
www.pbs.org/wgbh/amex/vietnam

The Vietnam War
www.vietnampix.com

The Wars for Vietnam: 1945 to 1975
vietnam.vassar.edu

Index